KILLING MR. GRIFFIN

by
Lois Duncan

Student Packet
Written by
Debbie Miller
Mary L. Dennis

Contains masters for:

1	Prereading Activity
4	Vocabulary Activities
4	Vocabulary Lists
1	Study Guide
4	Vocabulary Quizzes
4	Comprehension Quizzes
1	Final Exam
1	Ideas for Projects and Essays

PLUS Detailed Answer Key

Note
The text used to prepare this guide was the Laurel Leaf Suspense softcover edition published by Bantam Doubleday Dell Publishing Group, © 1978 by Lois Duncan. The page references may differ in other editions.

Please note: Please assess the appropriateness of this book for the age level and maturity of your students prior to reading and discussing it with your class.

ISBN 1-56137-343-5

Copyright 2000 by Novel Units, Inc., San Antonio, Texas. All rights reserved. No part of this publication may be reproduced, stored in a retrieval system, or transmitted in any way or by any means (electronic, mechanical, photocopying, recording, or otherwise) without prior written permission from Novel Units, Inc., with the following exceptions:

Photocopying of student worksheets by a teacher who purchased this publication for his/her own class is permissible. Reproduction of any part of this publication for an entire school or for a school system or for commercial sale is strictly prohibited. **Copyright infringement is a violation of federal law.**

Printed in the United States of America.

To order, contact your local school supply store, or—

Novel Units, Inc.
P.O. Box 791610
San Antonio, TX 78279

Web site: www.educyberstor.com

Name_____

Killing Mr. Griffin
Student Worksheet #1
Prereading Activity

Anticipation Guide

Answer each of the following questions in an organized, thoughtful way. Be sure to use complete sentences.

1. What is peer pressure? Give an example of peer pressure you felt in elementary school.

   _____
   _____
   _____
   _____
   _____

2. Describe a time when you did or were tempted to do something you knew was wrong because of peer pressure. Try to analyze what you thought about as you were trying to decide if you would go along with your friends. If you did choose to do what they wanted, tell how you felt about it afterwards.

   _____
   _____
   _____
   _____
   _____

3. Can peer pressure be positive as well as negative? Give some examples to support your opinion.

   _____
   _____
   _____
   _____
   _____

4. List three negative things a teenager might be pressured by peers to do. Tell how you would handle each situation, assuming you **do not** want to go along with the group.

   _____
   _____
   _____
   _____
   _____

© Novel Units, Inc.   All rights reserved

Name_____

Killing Mr. Griffin
Student Worksheet #2
Vocabulary—Chapters 1 & 2
Use With List 1

Word Maps

There are 24 words on Vocabulary List 1 (page 9). Your group will be responsible for mapping four of the words and then sharing the maps with the other groups. Everyone in your group should work on the maps for all four definitions. You will need a dictionary to find the definitions, a thesaurus to find the synonyms and antonyms, and everyone's imagination to write an interesting context sentence that shows you know what the words mean. Two maps are provided for you. Use the back of your paper to draw the remaining two maps.

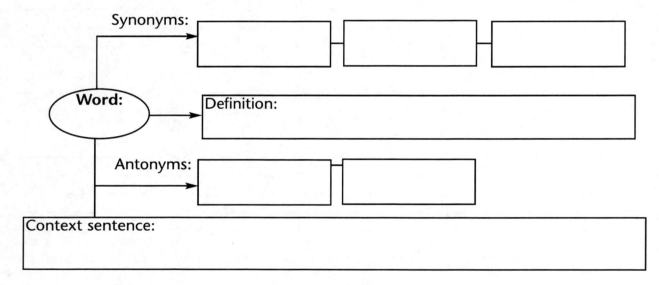

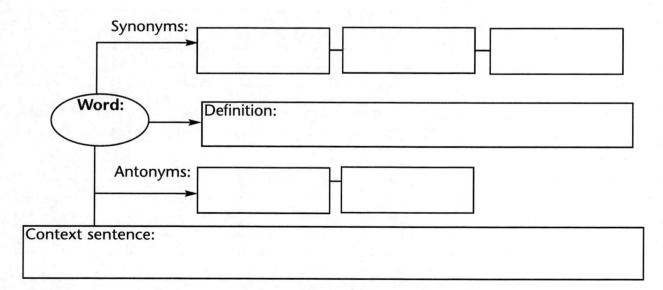

© Novel Units, Inc. All rights reserved

Name_____

Killing Mr. Griffin
Student Worksheet #3—page 1
Vocabulary —Chapters 3-8
Use With List 2

In Other Words...

Find the word from Vocabulary List 2 (page 10) that belongs in each blank. Write the word on the first blank line. Then, on the parenthetical blank, write another word that could be used to give the sentence the same meaning.

1. All the old pleasures _____ (_____).

2. His lips curled _____ (_____).

3. Under the kitchen window, the first _____ (_____) were blooming.

4. Her eyes brightened in _____ (_____).

5. "You can't _____ (_____) something like that."

6. Never, Susan thought _____ (_____), never in all the time to come will I ever, ever be as happy as I am right now.

7. "She's not a _____ (_____)."

8. The policeman, whom she had hoped to charm into letting her off with a warning, had not been _____ (_____).

9. "It would set a _____ (_____)."

10. She didn't know the woman's name, but she did know that she was _____ (_____).

11. ...she found herself the only one in the class excluded from Betsy's tenth birthday party, and was thereafter totally _____ (_____).

12. Her _____ (_____) liked her for her sparkle and charm.

13. As soon as he allowed such a _____ (_____) to cross his mind, he was swept with guilt.

© Novel Units, Inc.   All rights reserved

Name_____

Killing Mr. Griffin
Student Worksheet #3 - page 2

14. If she were to remove the blindfold, she knew she would find beneath it the policeman's cold, _____ (_____) stare.

15. "It won't _____ (_____)," said Mr. Griffin.

16. "I'm not going soft," Jeff said _____ (_____).

17. Perhaps it was because, _____ (_____) as she was, she never got exposed to any germs.

18. "Many of the kids coming into my classes at the university are all but _____ (_____)."

19. …David knew a strange, _____ (_____) sense of freedom.

20. To him she had been no more than a _____ (_____) shy little mouse of a girl…

21. Unless she remarried, her life was at a _____ (_____).

22. Now that she had been given permission, some _____ (_____) in her personality kept her from doing it.

23. There were only two people she knew who seemed _____ (_____) to Betsy's cuteness, and one was Mr. Griffin.

24. "I have an _____ (_____) personality."

25. There was a brief, _____ (_____) knock.

Name_____

Killing Mr. Griffin
Student Worksheet #4
Vocabulary—Chapters 9-14
Use With List 3

A Mystery for You to Solve

Use the words from Vocabulary List 3 (page 11) to fill in the blank squares below. Then read down the center to find the clue for the "What is it?" The answer to the "What is it?" can be found somewhere in your book. When you find it, write it on the line.

walking purposefully

extremely painful

not needing anything else

stronghold

dependable; upstanding

with sincere apology

thinking of something else

with doubt

with hard work and attention

frustration

[FREE]

lessen

heart condition

concerned; worried

serious crime

viewing the past

sadly

What is it?

CLUE: _____

Answer: _____

Name_____

KIlling Mr. Griffin
Student Worksheet #5
Vocabulary—Chapters 15-19
Use With List 4

Fit the words from Vocabulary List 4 (page 12) into the framework below. Then use a separate sheet of paper to write a clue for each word in the puzzle.

© Novel Units, Inc.

All rights reserved

Name_____   **Killing Mr. Griffin**
                                          Vocabulary List 1

Chapter 1

obscured 5 _____

vehemently 5 _____

staggered 8 _____

sophistication 9 _____

femme fatale 9 _____

accustomed 10 _____

conspiratorial 10 _____

inaudible 11 _____

rummaged 11 _____

saunter 12 _____

uncompromising 12 _____

disclosure 13 _____

alienated 13 _____

deceptively 15 _____

contemplate 15 _____

Chapter 2

contritely 18 _____

taut 19 _____

federal offense 20 _____

persecution complex 22 _____

decoy 22 _____

appraising 24 _____

luminosity 27 _____

ethereal 27 _____

transformation 27 _____

© Novel Units, Inc.   All rights reserved

Name_____

Killing Mr. Griffin
Vocabulary List 2

Chapter 3
conjecture 30 _____
wryly 31 _____
stalemate 35 _____
cloistered 35 _____

Chapter 4
perfunctory 43 _____
deliriously 51 _____

Chapter 5
contrariness 53 _____
illiterate 55 _____
abrasive 56 _____
hyacinths 56 _____
perfectionist 57 _____
precedent 58 _____

Chapter 6
slothful 62 _____
anticipation 63 _____
diminished 64 _____
regulate 67 _____

Chapter 7
susceptible 74 _____
ostracized 75 _____
contemporaries 76 _____
immune 76 _____
detonate 83 _____
insolent 84 _____
defensively 87 _____

Chapter 8
exhilarating 95 _____
studious 100 _____

© Novel Units, Inc.   All rights reserved

Name_____

Killing Mr. Griffin
Vocabulary List 3

Chapter 9
felony 109 _____

Chapter 10
agonizing 116 _____
mournfully 119 _____
angina 122 _____
preoccupied 123 _____
self-contained 123 _____

Chapter 11
fortress 129 _____
striding 129 _____
alleviate 130 _____

Chapter 12
retrospect 143 _____
stolid 144 _____

Chapter 13
disconcerted 152 _____
confrontation 158 _____
laboriously 159 _____

Chapter 14
exasperation 160 _____
contritely 168 _____
skeptically 169 _____

Name_____

Killing Mr. Griffin
Vocabulary List 4

Chapter 15
incredulous 173 _____
glowering 181 _____

Chapter 16
vulnerable _____
vial 185 _____
oblivion 189 _____
innate 194 _____
feigned 194 _____

Chapter 17
oppressive 197 _____
wake 201 _____
alibi 202 _____

Chapter 18
immobile 209 _____
bravado 214 _____

Chapter 19
lethargy 219 _____
callous 219 _____
impulsive 219 _____
thwarted 219 _____
plausible 219 _____
rationalizations 219 _____
clinical 220 _____
psychopath 220 _____
state's evidence 220 _____

© Novel Units, Inc.   All rights reserved

Name_____

Killing Mr. Griffin
Study Guide • page 1

Chapters 1 and 2

1. Describe the setting. Where and when does the story take place?

   _____
   _____
   _____
   _____

2. Describe the mood in Chapter 1.

   _____
   _____
   _____
   _____

3. In a well-written paragraph, describe Susan. Include a physical description, how she acts in class, and how she feels about her life. Would you want her for a friend? Explain why or why not?

   _____
   _____
   _____
   _____
   _____
   _____
   _____
   _____
   _____
   _____
   _____
   _____
   _____
   _____
   _____
   _____
   _____

Name_____

Killing Mr. Griffin
Study Guide • page 2

4. What excuse did each of the following give for not turning in their assignments?
   (a) Betsy _____
   _____
   (b) Jeff _____
   _____
   (c) David _____
   _____

5. Why does Mark dislike Mr. Griffin? _____
   _____
   _____
   _____
   _____
   _____

6. What was the secret plan discussed by the students? _____
   _____
   _____
   _____
   _____

7. Describe Mark's face as he revealed his plan. _____
   _____
   _____
   _____

8. When had Jeff seen the same expression on Mark's face in the past?
   _____
   _____
   _____

9. From what you know so far, what is your opinion of Mark? Would you want to be friends with him? Why or why not? _____
   _____
   _____
   _____
   _____
   _____

© Novel Units, Inc.   All rights reserved

Name_____

Killing Mr. Griffin
Study Guide • page 3

Chapters 3 and 4

10. Describe Dave. What are his responsibilities at home? What kind of student is he? What are his hopes for the future? Would you want to have Dave for a friend? Explain why or why not. _____
_____
_____
_____
_____
_____

11. Dave is unsure about helping Mark with his scheme. What does Mark say to convince him? _____
_____
_____

12. Who calls Sue? Why? _____
_____
_____
_____

13. What is Sue's reaction to her phone call? _____
_____
_____

14. What will be Sue's part in Mark's plan? _____
_____

15. What is Sue's initial reaction to the plan? Why does she finally agree?
_____
_____

16. What kind of feeling do you get from the last sentence of the chapter? The sentence is an example of what writing technique? _____
_____
_____
_____

Name_____

Killing Mr. Griffin
Study Guide • 4

Chapters 5 & 6

17. Imagine you are Brian Griffin's wife. Write a paragraph describing your husband.

_____
_____
_____
_____
_____
_____
_____
_____
_____
_____
_____
_____
_____

18. How does reading Mrs. Griffin's point of view change your perception of Mr. Griffin? _____
_____
_____
_____
_____
_____
_____

19. Why does Dave make the green Jell-O for his grandmother? Be specific.
_____
_____
_____

20. What alibi did Betsy, Mark, and Jeff arrange? Did everything go as planned?
_____
_____
_____
_____
_____
_____

Name_____   ***Killing Mr. Griffin***
                                          Study Guide • page 5

Chapters 7 and 8

21. How did Betsy try to talk the policeman out of giving her a speeding ticket? Did it work? _____
_____
_____
_____

22. Write a paragraph describing Betsy. What do you like/dislike about her? Would you want her for a friend? Explain why or why not. _____
_____
_____
_____
_____
_____
_____
_____
_____
_____
_____

23. What two people in Betsy's life are not influenced by her smile and charm?
_____

24. How do the students torment Brian Griffin in this chapter? _____
_____
_____
_____
_____

25. How does Susan react to learning that Mr. Griffin was left at the waterfall?
_____
_____

Name_____

Killing Mr. Griffin
Study Guide • page 6

Chapters 9 and 10

26. Why does it become so important for Dave and Sue to find Mark?
_____
_____
_____
_____

27. Mark is against revealing Mr. Griffin's death. What does he give as his reason? What is wrong with it?
_____
_____
_____
_____
_____

28. What have Mark's aunt and uncle done for him? Why does his uncle consider him weird? _____
_____
_____
_____
_____

29. What upset David so much in Chapter 10? _____
_____
_____
_____

30. What is ironic about David's grandmother's description of going to sleep like Snow White? _____
_____
_____
_____
_____

31. How does Detective Baca react when Kathy Griffin reports her husband missing?
_____
_____
_____
_____

Name_____

Killing Mr. Griffin
Study Guide • page 7

Chapters 11 and 12

32. Why is it especially important for Susan to show up at school?
_____
_____
_____

33. What did Mark instruct Susan to say when she was called down to the office? What was his logic? _____
_____
_____

34. At this point in the story, do (or did) you think Susan would be capable of lying convincingly? Why or why not? _____
_____
_____

35. What do you think will happen next? _____
_____
_____

36. Describe the body when the students came back to it. _____
_____
_____
_____

37. Why is Betsy so critical of Sue? _____
_____
_____
_____

38. Who participates in digging the grave? What goes through their minds as they dig? _____
_____
_____

39. How does Mark act as the grave is being dug? _____
_____
_____

© Novel Units, Inc.   All rights reserved

Name_____

Killing Mr. Griffin
Study Guide • page 8

Chapters 13 and 14

40. Why is Mrs. Griffin so sure Sue is lying about the blond woman? What analogy does she make? _____
_____
_____

41. How does Sue's attitude toward her family change? Why? _____
_____
_____

42. What does Mrs. Griffin remember about
    (a) Dave _____
    _____
    (b) Mark _____
    _____

43. How does the detective get the medicine vial and find the body? _____
_____
_____
_____
_____

44. Why is Mark so angry at Betsy about her speeding ticket? _____
_____
_____

45. Why did the students think they were being tricked when they heard reports that the body had been found? _____
_____
_____

46. What was the plan to get rid of Mr. Griffin's car? _____
_____
_____
_____
_____

Name_____

Killing Mr. Griffin
Study Guide • page 9

Chapters 15 and 16

47. How did Dave explain taking Mr. Griffin's ring? What do we know that Dave and Sue don't? _____
_____
_____
_____

48. Why didn't Grandma Ruggles believe what Dave and Sue told her about finding the ring? Where did she think David had gotten it? _____
_____
_____
_____

49. Who did Sue call when she got home? What do you think she said?
_____
_____
_____

50. How do Jeff's parents feel about Mark? Where do you think they got their information? _____
_____
_____
_____

51. Why did Irma Ruggles refuse to attend church?_____
_____
_____
_____
_____

52. Who came to Grandma Ruggles' room while Dave and his mother were at church? _____

Name_____ **Killing Mr. Griffin**
Study Guide • page 10

Chapters 17 and 18

53. According to the autopsy, how did Brian Griffin die? _____
_____

54. Why do Jeff and Betsy come over to Sue's house? _____
_____
_____

55. After Sue talks to Dave on the phone, what does she conclude? _____
_____

56. When Sue revealed what she had learned to Jeff and Betsy, what was their reaction? Who did Betsy go and get? _____
_____

57. What is Mark's explanation for Grandma Ruggles' death? _____
_____
_____

58. Who shows a definite concern about how Mark will make certain Sue doesn't talk? _____
_____

59. What do we discover about the death of Mark's father? _____
_____

60. Who saved Sue, and why is this ironic? _____
_____

Chapter 19

61. What are the personality characteristics of a psychopath? _____
_____
_____

62. What does "turning in state's evidence" mean? _____
_____
_____

63. On the back of your paper, write a paragraph explaining how the decision to go along with Mark's plan changed forever the lives of Betsy, Jeff, Dave, and Sue.

© Novel Units, Inc.   All rights reserved

Name_____

Killing Mr. Griffin
Vocabulary Quiz
Chapters 1 and 2

Write the letter of the correct definition next to each vocabulary word.

_____ 1. vehemently
_____ 2. uncompromising
_____ 3. contritely
_____ 4. sophistication
_____ 5. ethereal
_____ 6. rummaged
_____ 7. deceptively
_____ 8. transformation
_____ 9. taut
_____ 10. obscured
_____ 11. accustomed
_____ 12. inaudible
_____ 13. alienated
_____ 14. staggered
_____ 15. appraising
_____ 16. saunter
_____ 17. federal offense
_____ 18. femme fatale
_____ 19. decoy
_____ 20. disclosure
_____ 21. contemplate
_____ 22. conspiratorial
_____ 23. luminosity
_____ 24. persecution complex

a. clouded
b. strongly
c. stumbled or walked erratically
d. wisdom of the world
e. attractive woman
f. expected
g. scheming
h. not loud enough to be heard
i. sorted through
j. walk slowly and casually
k. steadfast
l. revelation
m. apart from others
n. sneakily
o. consider
p. with sincere regret
q. tight
r. major crime
s. feeling that one is being mistreated
t. bait
u. evaluating
v. brilliance
w. insubstantial
x. complete change

© Novel Units, Inc.   All rights reserved

Name_____

Killing Mr. Griffin
Comprehension Quiz
Chapters 1-5

Circle the letter of the best response.

1. The setting of the novel is
   a. modern New Mexico
   b. modern New York
   c. the Old West
   d. California, 1973

2. Susan McConnell often dreamed of
   a. sharing private thoughts with David
   b. dating Jeff Garrett
   c. living alone by a lake
   d. a and c

3. Mark was the <u>most</u> angry at Mr. Griffin for
   a. not accepting late assignments
   b. making him beg to retake the class
   c. assigning difficult homework
   d. being taken in by Betsy's charm

4. The students who originally planned Mr. Griffin's kidnapping were
   a. Betsy, Mark, and Jeff
   b. David, Sue, and Betsy
   c. Jeff, Mark, and David
   d. Mark, Jeff, and Sue

5. All of the following describe Dave's home and family <u>except</u>
   a. a grandmother who required his care and company after school
   b. housework that he shared with his mother
   c. a neglectful mother who forget to buy food for lunch
   d. high expectations for Dave's future success

6. The reason Dave called Sue and asked her for a date was that
   a. he had always wanted to do something wild.
   b. he had admired her for a long time, but was too shy to call.
   c. it was part of the plan to use Sue as a decoy.
   d. he needed a date for the picnic.

7. On the picnic, Mark did all of the following <u>except</u>
   a. drank beer
   b. led the group to the spot by the falls
   c. smoked pot
   d. swam in the river

8. Kathy Griffin is
   a. Mr. Griffin's mother
   b. Mr. Griffin's wife
   c. Mr. Griffin's sister
   d. Mr. Griffin's grandmother

9. Mr. Griffin became a high school teacher because
   a. he was shocked at the incompetence of university students
   b. he was unable to keep up with other college professors
   c. when he moved from Michigan, it was the only job he could get
   d. he was writing a book about teaching in a public school

10. Kathy urged Brian to
    a. give up teaching
    b. remember to pick up his pills
    c. offer praise as well as criticism
    d. none of these

© Novel Units, Inc. All rights reserved

Name_____

Killing Mr. Griffin
Vocabulary Quiz
Chapters 3-8

Circle the letter of the correct definition below each word.

1. conjecture
   a. thought
   b. connection
   c. conjunction

2. wry
   a. bread
   b. natural
   c. ironic

3. stalemate
   a. progression
   b. standstill
   c. partner

4. cloistered
   a. ill
   b. confined
   c. bedridden

5. perfunctory
   a. meaningless
   b. percussive
   c. anticipated

6. deliriously
   a. deliciously
   b. delicately
   c. excitedly

7. contrariness
   a. stubbornness
   b. perversity
   c. stupidity

8. illiterate
   a. not able to read
   b. not able to write
   c. a and b

9. abrasive
   a. pleasant
   b. difficult
   c. strange

10. hyacinths
    a. written words
    b. coded words
    c. spring flowers

11. perfectionist
    a. stickler
    b. dare-devil
    c. performer

12. precedent
    a. previous event
    b. high official
    c. part of speech

13. anticipation
    a. heart condition
    b. antidote
    c. expectation

14. diminished
    a. increased
    b. discussed
    c. lessened

15. regulate
    a. control
    b. kinship
    c. relegate

16. susceptible
    a. excluded
    b. observable
    c. vulnerable

17. ostracized
    a. capsized
    b. exploded
    c. shut out

18. contemporaries
    a. thinkers
    b. peers
    c. temporary pals

19. immune
    a. intelligent
    b. susceptible
    c. unaffected

20. detonate
    a. discolor
    b. explode
    c. irregularity

21. insolent
    a. poor
    b. lazy
    c. rude

22. defensively
    a. protectively
    b. selfishly
    c. perfectly

23. exhilarating
    a. persuasive
    b. invigorating
    c. evil

24. studious
    a. smooth
    b. negligent
    c. scholarly

25. slothful
    a. intellectual
    b. lazy
    c. silly

Name_____

Killing Mr. Griffin
Comprehension Quiz
Chapters 6-10

Match the letter next to each character with the action for which he/she was responsible.

a. Susan
b. David
c. Irma Ruggles
d. Mark
e. Betsy
f. David's mother
g. Jeff
h. James Baca
i. Kathy Griffin
j. Liz Cline
k. Mr. Griffin

_____ 1. doctored green Jell-O with sleeping pills
_____ 2. told fellow bridge players how wonderful her daughter is
_____ 3. made an appointment to talk to Mr. Griffin about her work
_____ 4. got a speeding ticket on the way to the school
_____ 5. warned Susan to run
_____ 6. was the only freshman to attend the senior prom
_____ 7. was the first to jump Mr. Griffin
_____ 8. found a vial of pills on the path
_____ 9. said, "Make him cry. I want to see him cry."
_____10. objected to leaving Mr. Griffin at the falls
_____11. insisted on going back to the falls the night of the kidnapping
_____12. was the first to realize Mr. Griffin was dead
_____13. announced that his father died in a fire
_____14. held and comforted a crying Sue
_____15. was unhappy to have missed her game shows
_____16. assigned to investigate Mr. Griffin's disappearance
_____17. attended Stanford University
_____18. refused to believe that Mr. Griffin ran away
_____19. implied that Mr. Griffin ran away because he was not ready for fatherhood
_____20. tried to referee the discussion about the Jell-O

© Novel Units, Inc.   All rights reserved

Name_____

Killing Mr. Griffin
Vocabulary Quiz
Chapters 9-14

Choose a word from the box to complete each sentence, and write it on the line.

felony	exasperation	preoccupied	striding
skeptically	angina	stolid	fortress
agonizing	laboriously	self-contained	
contritely	retrospect	disconcerted	
mournfully	confrontation	alleviate	

1. Watching the team lose was a(n) _____ experience.
2. Before he was 16, he had already committed a(n) _____.
3. From their campsite, they could hear the wolves howling _____.
4. He always carried his pills in case of a(n) _____ attack.
5. Sarah's father, a professor, often seems _____ with his reading.
6. They rented a(n) _____ camper and drove to Alaska.
7. During the early days in America, a(n) _____ provided protection.
8. The shoplifters were _____ through the store, trying to look like regular customers.
9. The medicine the doctor gave her did little to _____ the pain.
10. Looking at it in_____, losing his job had been a good thing.
11. Her parents were _____ church and community members.
12. Although he was _____ by the vocabulary portion of the test, he knew he had done well on the math.
13. Kate went home the back way to avoid a(n) _____ with Jason's old girl friend.
14. They had _____ cleaned the graffiti off the walls using the toothbrushes the principal gave them.
15. The teacher's _____ grew as she realized the students were only thinking of the upcoming vacation.
16. Because he had apologized _____ for missing practice, the coach gave him another chance.
17. "Might as well not bother with the picnic lunch," he said, looking _____ at the grey rain clouds.

Name_____

Killing Mr. Griffin
Comprehension Quiz
Chapters 11-14

Write "True" if the statement is true. Write "False" if the statement is false.

_____ 1. The students called Miss Luna "Dolly" even though she didn't like it.
_____ 2. Susan was surprised when she was called to the office.
_____ 3. Jeff told Susan exactly what lies to tell the authorities.
_____ 4. Sue was not present when Mr. Griffin's body was buried.
_____ 5. It was David's idea to take the cash from Mr. Griffin's wallet.
_____ 6. It was Mark's idea to use the credit cards to make it look as though Mr. Griffin had left town.
_____ 7. Betsy was jealous of the way Mark treated Sue.
_____ 8. David and Jeff were the only ones who dug the grave.
_____ 9. Betsy drove Mr. Griffin's car to the airport.
_____ 10. Mrs. Griffin believed the story Susan told about Mr. Griffin.
_____ 11. Susan recalled that Mr. Griffin was wearing a watch.
_____ 12. Mrs. Griffin remembered that Jeff had copied a term paper from someone at the university.
_____ 13. David acted strangely at home because he was secretly seeing his father.
_____ 14. Sue finally turned in the empty pill bottle to Detective Baca.
_____ 15. Mark made all the decisions about how to carry out the plan and then how to cover up what happened.

Identify each speaker by matching the quote with the correct letter.

a. Mark   b. David   c. Betsy   d. Jeff   e. Sue

_____ 16. "He said that I was spoiled—that we were all spoiled—because we're used to overgrading."

_____ 17. "Whose girl friend are you, anyway, Mark's or mine?"

_____ 18. "Can you think of a better way to get rid of a car than to have somebody steal it?"

_____ 19. "Our luck's run out on us. There's a police car behind us."

_____ 20. "Ugh—it's grotesque. I'm going downstream and sit and watch the water."

© Novel Units, Inc.   All rights reserved

Name_____

Killing Mr. Griffin
Vocabulary Quiz
Chapters 15-19

Write the letter of the correct definition next to each vocabulary word.

_____ 1. incredulous
_____ 2. impulsive
_____ 3. lethargy
_____ 4. oppressive
_____ 5. thwarted
_____ 6. wake
_____ 7. glowering
_____ 8. psychopath
_____ 9. alibi
_____ 10. vulnerable
_____ 11. plausible
_____ 12. immobile
_____ 13. vial
_____ 14. rationalizations
_____ 15. bravado
_____ 16. oblivion
_____ 17. callous
_____ 18. clinical
_____ 19. innate
_____ 20. state's evidence
_____ 21. feigned

a. skeptical
b. glaring
c. susceptible
d. small bottle
e. disregard or extinction
f. born with
g. pretended
h. abusive
i. deathwatch
j. excuse
k. not moving
l. boasting
m. lack of energy
n. unfeeling
o. sudden; not thought out
p. prevented
q. possible; believable
r. justifications
s. scientific
t. psychotic individual
u. information needed to convict a felon

Name_____

Killing Mr. Griffin
Comprehension Quiz
Chapters 15-19

Put the following sets of events in chronological order, numbering each set 1-5. Then put the sets themselves in chronological order, lettering A-D.

☐ ____ 1. Sue must listen to her parents discuss the murder.
  ____ 2. Mark pays a visit to Grandma Ruggles.
  ____ 3. Jeff's parents discuss Mark.
  ____ 4. Dave and his mother go to church.
  ____ 5. Grandma Ruggles admits to herself the ring is not her son's.

☐ ____ 1. Mark sets the curtains on fire.
  ____ 2. Mrs. McConnell explains to Sue that Mark is a psychopath.
  ____ 3. Kathy Griffin and Detective Baca rescue Sue.
  ____ 4. Jeff and Betsy help Mark tie up Sue.
  ____ 5. Sue tells Jeff, Betsy, and Mark how much she hates them.

☐ ____ 1. David introduces Sue to his grandmother.
  ____ 2. Sue tries to help David lie about the ring.
  ____ 3. David goes to his house with Sue to get the ring.
  ____ 4. Sue calls Mark.
  ____ 5. David offers to give Grandma Ruggles a dozen candy bars in exchange for the ring.

☐ ____ 1. Sue decides not to accompany her family to the church supper.
  ____ 2. Betsy wants Sue to be her alibi for the night.
  ____ 3. Sue realizes Mark killed Grandma Ruggles.
  ____ 4. Jeff and Betsy pay a surprise visit to Sue.
  ____ 5. A phone call to David reveals that Gram is dead.

Name_____

Killing Mr. Griffin
Final Exam

Choose the best answer.

1. Who is the author of the novel, *Killing Mr. Griffin*?
   a. Zindell   b. Duncan   c. Ross   d. Luis

2. Where does the story take place?
   a. Florida   b. California   c. New Mexico   d. Texas

3. Whose idea was it originally to kill Mr. Griffin?
   a. Mark   b. Dave   c. Jeff   d. Sue

4. What did Mark do as a child to make us believe he was capable of murder?
   a. vandalized homes   b. set fire to a cat   c. pulled the wings off a bird

5. How did Mark's father die?
   a. car accident   b. suicide   c. heart attack   d. fire

Match the character with the description.

   a. Mark   b. Sue   c. Betsy   d. Dave   e. Jeff

_____ 6. told Mr. Griffin the assignment blew away

_____ 7. claimed not to understand the assignment

_____ 8. president of the senior class

_____ 9. a shy, bespectacled girl

_____ 10. a basketball player

_____ 11. had a crush on Mark

_____ 12. had a crush on Dave

_____ 13. got everywhere with her smile

_____ 14. had no signs of remorse after the death of Mr. Griffin

_____ 15. was not present when Mr. Griffin was kidnapped

Name_____

Killing Mr. Griffin
Final Exam • 2

Choose the best answer.

16. What was the purpose of involving Dave in the scheme?
    a. to be used as a decoy
    b. to get Sue involved in the scheme
    c. because he is the class president
    d. because he has no father

17. Who was used as the decoy?
    a. Mark   b. Dave   c. Betsy   d. Sue

18. What did Dave's father and Mr. Griffin have in common?
    a. both ran away from responsibility
    b. both attended Stanford University
    c. both disliked kids
    d. nothing at all

19. At the picnic, what finally convinced Sue to become part of the plan?
    a. Mark pleaded
    b. Dave bribed her
    c. Dave kissed her on the forehead
    d. Betsy said she'd be her best friend

20. Why did Mr. Griffin leave his job at the university?
    a. wanted to make an impression on high school students
    b. got fired from his college job
    c. got paid more for teaching high school
    d. didn't receive tenure

21. David provided himself with an alibi by
    a. staying after school
    b. drugging his grandmother
    c. putting his voice on tape at Betsy's
    d. helping decorate for a dance

22. Betsy, Jeff, and Mark's alibi included all of the following except
    a. a tape recorder   b. a chocolate cake   c. sleeping pills   d. telephone

23. Why was Betsy late to the kidnapping?
    a. It was part of the plan.
    b. She lost the car keys.
    c. She had second thoughts.
    d. She got a speeding ticket.

24. When the bag went over Mr. Griffin's face, what did he yell to Sue?
    a. "What's going on?"
    b. "I'll get you for this."
    c. "Help!"
    d. "Run!"

25. After the discovery of Mr. Griffin's body, who wanted to tell somebody?
    a. Dave   b. Sue   c. Betsy   d. Jeff

Name_____

Killing Mr. Griffin
Final Exam • 3

26. What was Mark's relationship with Lana Turnboldt?
    a. She was an old flame who gave him a term paper to copy.
    b. She is really his sister.
    c. They were in the same history class.
    d. None of these.

27. What two people were not affected by Betsy's "cuteness"?
    a. Sue and Dave   c. Jeff and Dave
    b. her mom and dad   d. Mr. Griffin and Mark

28. Who closed Mr. Griffin's eyes before the burial?
    a. Betsy   b. Dave   c. Mark   d. Jeff

29. Who drove Mr. Griffin's car to the airport?
    a. Betsy   b. Dave   c. Jeff   d. Mark

30. Irma Ruggles believed David was seeing his father because
    a. she found the Stanford ring.   c. David had been acting funny.
    b. she caught Dave and Sue in a lie. d. all of the above.

True or False

_____ 31. Mark Kinney hated Mr. Griffin because he sent him to the office.
_____ 32. The students intended to kill Mr. Griffin.
_____ 33. Sue and Jeff discovered that Mr. Griffin was dead.
_____ 34. While digging the grave, Mark was very remorseful.
_____ 35. Mark painted Mr. Griffin's car to disguise it.
_____ 36. Jeff's parents thought Mark had a terrible home life.
_____ 37. During the kidnapping, Jeff put the bag over Mr. Griffin's head.
_____ 38. Mr. Griffin regarded Dolly Luna as a 30-year-old teenager.
_____ 39. Dave's mother was highly regarded at her church.
_____ 40. Dave's grandmother refused to go to church because of a sermon.
_____ 41. A plastic vial led the police to the grave.
_____ 42. Dave's windbreaker was an important piece of evidence.
_____ 43. Mark convinced everyone to do what he wanted by manipulation.
_____ 44. Betsy was jealous of Sue because of the treatment she received from Mark.
_____ 45. Mr. Griffin was really Dave's father who disappeared years ago.

Name_____

Killing Mr. Griffin
Final Exam • 4

Match each word with its definition.

_____ 46. angina
_____ 47. illiterate
_____ 48. feign
_____ 49. conjecture
_____ 50. immobile
_____ 51. alibi
_____ 52. vehemently
_____ 53. cloistered
_____ 54. femme fatale
_____ 55. perfunctory
_____ 56. vulnerable
_____ 57. abrasive
_____ 58. saunter
_____ 59. transformation
_____ 60. thwarted

a. not moving
b. strongly
c. excuse
d. meaningless; routine
e. walk slowly
f. change in form
g. pretend
h. prevented
i. unable to read or write
j. attractive woman
k. heart problem
l. secluded
m. easily led or hurt
n. harsh; rough
o. guess or consideration

Essay. Choose two of the questions below, and write a well-developed paragraph for each one. Be sure to identify the questions you are answering, and use examples from the novel to support your statements.

A. In what ways did peer pressure affect the characters in the book?

B. How were the parents in the novel deceived or "blind" to what their children were really doing?

C. What are the characteristics of a psychopath, and how did Mark show that he had these characteristics?

© Novel Units, Inc. All rights reserved

Name_____

Ideas for Projects and Essays

1. With a small group, dramatize a scene from the novel.

2. Draw a scene from the story using charcoal, water colors, or pastels.

3. On poster board, make a collage showing some of the things teens are pressured into by peers. Be sure to include positive as well as negative things.

4. Write the next chapter of the story. It occurs six months after the trial. Through dialogue between two or more of the characters, explain what has happened to all of the students involved in the kidnapping scheme.

5. Find out more about psychopaths. In the newspaper, look for examples of acts committed by people you believe are psychopaths. Give a short oral report.

6. Write the newspaper article which appeared the day after the police found Mr. Griffin's body. You might include interviews with Mrs. Griffin, another teacher, and Lana Turnboldt.

7. Write a brief speech that Mr. Griffin's principal might give at his funeral.

8. Write a paper comparing and contrasting Dave's home life with Sue's.

9. Imagine you were one of the students in the story. Devise a different plan for letting Mr. Griffin know the students are upset about his grading policies and homework.

10. Discuss, in a short essay, how your impression of Mark changed from the beginning to the end of the novel.

11. Change the story: Mr. Griffin is taken back to town as originally planned. Except for a few bruises, he is unharmed. Although he didn't see any of the students involved, he has a pretty good idea who some of them were. What happens next?

12. Read another book by Lois Duncan. Compare the characters and plot with those of *Killing Mr. Griffin*.

13. Write an essay explaining why you think Mark is a psychopath. Imagine you are the judge at his trial. What sentence would you give him? Why?

14. Compare Mr. Griffin with a similar teacher you have had. Hard work and frustration aside, did you learn a lot in your "tough" teacher's class? Do you think Mr. Griffin was a good teacher? If not, how might he have changed?

Answer Key

Student Worksheets:

#1: Student answers will vary, but should be discussed with the class as a whole.

#2: Teacher Note: Divide the class into six equal teams. Each team should be responsible for four words. Once the groups have finished their maps, they can trade with another group, or you can have two groups work together to exchange information.

#3: Synonyms given as second answers will vary, but first answers should match those below. Samples for second answers are given.

1. diminished (lessened)
2. wryly (ironically)
3. hyacinths (spring flowers)
4. anticipation (expectation)
5. regulate (control)
6. deliriously (excitedly)
7. perfectionist (stickler)
8. susceptible (easily influenced)
9. precedent (trend)
10. slothful (lazy)
11. ostracized (ignored)
12. contemporaries (peers)
13. conjecture (thought)
14. insolent (rude)
15. detonate (explode)
16. defensively (protectively)
17. cloistered (secluded)
18. illiterate (unable to read or write)
19. exhilarating (invigorating)
20. studious (scholarly)
21. stalemate (standstill)
22. contrariness (stubbornness)
23. immune (unaffected)
24. abrasive (harsh)
25. perfunctory (meaningless)

#4: Words from top to bottom are: STRIDING, AGONIZING, SELF-CONTAINED, FORTRESS, STOLID, CONTRITELY, PREOCCUPIED, SKEPTICALLY, LABORIOUSLY, EXASPERATION, ALLEVIATE, ANGINA, DISCONCERTED, FELONY, RETROSPECT, MOURNFULLY. The clue is DON'T LOOK BEHIND YOU. The answer is: another novel by the same author, Lois Duncan. (Found on second page inside front cover.)

#5:

1. rationalizations (justifications)
2. callous (unfeeling)
3. (across) vial (small bottle)
4. (down) vulnerable (easily hurt or led)
5. incredulous (unbelieving)
6. clinical (scientific)
7. immobile (not moving)
8. innate (inborn)
9. (across) oblivion (extinction)
10. (down) oppressive (abusive)
11. thwarted (prevented)
12. alibi (excuse)
13. feigned (pretended)
14. bravado (boasting)
15. glowering (glaring)
16. state's evidence (information the state needs to convict a criminal)
17. lethargy (lack of energy)
18. wake (deathwatch)
19. impulsive (not thought out)
20. psychopath (sociopath; antisocial)
21. plausible (believable; possible)

Study Guide

1. The dusty red plains of New Mexico near the Sandia Mountains is the setting. Published in 1978, the novel is set in the mid 1970s.
2. Susan, who is shy and studious, is feeling sorry for herself. The mood is negative and depressed.
3. Susan is skinny and wears glasses. She dreams of David, the class president, but has little hope of ever being the kind of beautiful, popular girl she thinks would attract him. She is an excellent student but very shy in class. She often wishes she could live alone by a lake, reading and writing.
4. Betsy: didn't understand the assignment; Jeff: had a basketball game; David: it blew away.
5. Mark is taking the English class for the second time. He had to beg Mr. Griffin to let him retake it.
6. Mark had the idea of kidnapping Mr. Griffin and threatening him in order to make sure they would pass English and graduate.
7. His face was strangely radiant and luminous.
8. when he set fire to a cat
9. Student opinions will vary, but should be supported with reasonable explanations.
10. Dave, senior class president, is an excellent student. He helps with housework and the care of his invalid grandmother. He feels he will have to support his mother and grandmother in the future, so he plans to go to law school on a scholarship.
11. Mark asks him how long it's been since he did something wild, just for fun. Since Dave is feeling a little sorry for himself, this is just what he needs to hear to convince him.
12. Dave calls Sue because she is needed as a decoy in the scheme.
13. She is deliriously happy and can hardly believe her good fortune.
14. She will make an appointment with Mr. Griffin to discuss her work, thereby detaining him while the others make preparations to grab him as he leaves the building.
15. She thinks the others are crazy, but the picnic and Dave's kiss convince her.
16. The author is using foreshadowing to imply that something bad will happen.
17. Students' descriptions will vary, but should include that Kathy saw her husband as a devoted and conscientious teacher who really cared about his students' education.
18. student opinion
19. She is fond of it, and he knows it will be the perfect vehicle for the sleeping pills with which he plans to drug her so that he can join the scheme.
20. Betsy called her mother, who was playing bridge at a friend's house, and made sure her mother heard the voices of the boys. She even tape-recorded the conversation. Then she made it look as though they had eaten three pieces of cake, and left the music playing loudly so that a neighbor would complain.
21. told him her father was on the County Commission
22. Betsy is cute and charming, and most adults think she is wonderful. In reality, she's a spoiled, selfish little snob.
23. Mark and Mr. Griffin
24. Mr. Griffin is kidnapped and taken to a secluded spot in the mountains. He is told by Mark that he is going to die.
25. She insists on going there to release him.
26. When they got to the waterfall, they found Mr. Griffin dead. Since Mark was in charge, they were relying on him to decide what to do next.

27. He says they will be tried as adults because kidnapping is a felony. He did not think through to the fact that they didn't actually kill him, and an autopsy would reveal this.
28. They have taken him in since his father died and his mother had a nervous breakdown. Mark is rarely home, and doesn't say anything when he is there.
29. His grandmother has some doubts about whether he was really there the previous afternoon.
30. Snow White went to sleep because of a drugged apple.
31. He implies that Mr. Griffin panicked about his impending fatherhood.
32. Everything must appear totally normal.
33. Mark told her to say that a beautiful young blond had been waiting for Mr. Griffin in his car. He thought everyone would think he had run away with her.
34. student opinion
35. student opinion
36. It was stiff, cold, and the eyes were open. Flies were crawling on it.
37. She is jealous because of the way Mark caters to Sue.
38. Jeff and Dave. Jeff jokes about being like one of the grave-diggers in *Hamlet*. Dave is more serious and concerned.
39. Mark acts like he is everyone's boss, and very worldly-wise about crime.
40. Mrs. Griffin knows her husband very well, and knows he would not act as Sue has said. She makes the analogy that she knows him as well as Sue's parents know her.
41. She realizes how much she loves them. The finality of death has made her appreciative of those she used to criticize for small faults which she now finds endearing.
42. Mrs. Griffin remembers that Dave reported his papers blew away, and that Mark copied a term paper.
43. Lana Turnboldt, Mark's old girl friend, found the pill vial and turned it in.
44. The alibi they had set up will be ruined if they are ever investigated.
45. Mark convinced them it was a trick, just to "get a reaction."
46. paint it in Jeff's garage and then abandon it in the desert
47. He felt it was something that belonged to him a long time ago. We know that Mr. Griffin and Dave's father both attended Stanford.
48. She thought it was her son's ring, and that David was secretly seeing his father.
49. Mark; student opinion
50. They feel Mark takes advantage of Jeff, but feel sorry for him because they have been told (probably by Mark) that his uncle beats him. They are truly "blind" parents.
51. The minister had preached against "those who refuse to shoulder their earthly burdens," and she took it personally.
52. Mark
53. an angina attack
54. to ask Sue to provide an alibi for Betsy while they take the car to Zuni
55. that Mark killed Grandma Ruggles
56. They didn't believe her. They got Mark.
57. She "fell."
58. Jeff
59. Mark set the fire.
60. Kathy Griffin and Detective Baca
61. See page 219 for a complete description.
62. providing evidence needed for the state to convict
63. Students' paragraphs will vary.

Vocabulary Quiz: Chapters 1 and 2

1. B	5. W	9. Q	13. M	17. R	21. O
2. K	6. I	10. A	14. C	18. E	22. G
3. P	7. N	11. F	15. U	19. T	23. V
4. D	8. X	12. H	16. J	20. L	24. S

Comprehension Quiz, Chapters 1-5

1. A
2. D
3. B
4. A
5. C
6. C
7. D
8. B
9. A
10. C

Vocabulary Quiz, Chapters 3-8

1. A
2. C
3. B
4. B
5. A
6. C
7. B
8. C
9. B
10. C
11. A
12. A
13. C
14. C
15. A
16. C
17. C
18. B
19. C
20. B
21. C
22. A
23. B
24. C
25. B

Comprehension Quiz, Chapters 6-10

1. B
2. J
3. A
4. E
5. K
6. E
7. G
8. E
9. E
10. B
11. A
12. B
13. D
14. D
15. C
16. H
17. K
18. I
19. H
20. F

Vocabulary Quiz, Chapters 9-14

1. agonizing
2. felony
3. mournfully
4. angina
5. preoccupied
6. self-contained
7. fortress
8. striding
9. alleviate
10. retrospect
11. stolid
12. disconcerted
13. confrontation
14. laboriously
15. exasperation
16. contritely
17. skeptically

Comprehension Quiz, Chapters 11-14

1. false
2. false
3. false
4. true
5. false
6. true
7. true
8. true
9. true
10. false
11. true
12. false
13. false
14. false
15. true
16. E
17. D
18. A
19. B
20. C

Vocabulary Quiz, Chapters 15-19

1. A
2. O
3. M
4. H
5. P
6. I
7. B
8. T
9. J
10. C
11. Q
12. K
13. D
14. R
15. L
16. E
17. N
18. S
19. F
20. U
21. G

Comprehension Quiz, Chapters 15-19
Events in sets from top to bottom:
1,5,2,3,4
3,5,4,1,2
2,4,1,5,3
1,3,5,2,4
Sets themselves, top to bottom: B,D,A,C

Final Exam

1. B
2. C
3. A
4. B
5. D
6. D
7. C
8. D
9. B
10. E
11. C
12. B
13. C
14. A
15. C
16. B
17. D
18. B
19. C
20. A
21. B
22. C
23. D
24. D
25. B
26. A
27. D
28. B
29. A
30. D
31. F
32. F
33. F
34. F
35. F
36. T
37. F
38. T
39. T
40. T
41. T
42. F
43. T
44. T
45. F
46. K
47. I
48. G
49. O
50. A
51. C
52. B
53. L
54. J
55. D
56. M
57. N
58. E
59. F
60. H